A Boat Ready to Set Sail

A Boat Ready to Set Sail

The Complete Poetical Works of

Pak Yong-chŏl

Translated by

Sung-Il Lee

RESOURCE *Publications* · Eugene, Oregon

A BOAT READY TO SET SAIL
The Complete Poetical Works of Pak Yong-chŏl

Copyright © 2024 Sung-Il Lee. All rights reserved. Except for brief quotations in critical publications or reviews, no part of this book may be reproduced in any manner without prior written permission from the publisher. Write: Permissions, Wipf and Stock Publishers, 199 W. 8th Ave., Suite 3, Eugene, OR 97401.

Wipf & Stock
An Imprint of Wipf and Stock Publishers
199 W. 8th Ave., Suite 3
Eugene, OR 97401

www.wipfandstock.com

PAPERBACK ISBN: 979-8-3852-2489-0
HARDCOVER ISBN: 979-8-3852-2490-6
EBOOK ISBN: 979-8-3852-2491-3

To the Memory of

Pak Yong-chŏl (1904–1938),

Whose name was writ in ink

Pak Yong-chŏl (박용철 1904–1938)

Contents

Preface   13
A Thank-you Note   14

Poems

A Boat Ready to Set Sail   17
After Sending You off on a Night Train   18
Though Unable to Go Away Like This   20
Chilled Forehead   21
Home   22
Whereto?   23
Rain   24
The Fairy's Song   25
Words of a Maiden Leaving for a Far-off Place   27
A Little Devil   29
Lines from 'The Soft Wings'   30
No Title   32
Hope and Despair   33
Rainy Day   34
From Despair   35
Be Nobler!   36
The Horse I Loved   37
As I'm Not Yours   38
An Owl is Hooting   39
A Grave and the Moon   41
A Heart Soaked with Rain   42
A Fragment of Thought (I)   43
A Fragment of Thought (II)   44
Title Lost (I)   45
Title Lost (II)   46
Winter Solstice   47
Oblivion   48
A Love-song   49

Sentimental 51
Renewed Happiness 52
Shiny Trace 53
I Commit Him to the Flame 54
Two Birds 55
Again 56
Satyrs 57
A Jolly Night 58
Title Lost (III) 59
Title Lost (IV) 60
Snow Falls 61
Upon the Sand on a Moonlit Night 62
Snow (I) 63
A Certain Night 64
Night 65
The Kite and the Blue Pool 66
A Song of the Listless Wind 67
Title Lost (V) 69
A Fracture of the Sky 70
Small Sky 71
Your Shadow 72
A Chance Encounter 73
A Clock That Has Stopped 74
A Doll 75
Mademoiselle Typist 76
Being in Love 77
Snow (II) 78
The Night before 79
The Vale of Ten-Thousand Waterfalls 81
Prayer 82
Invocation 83
Our Nursing Mom (*The Boy's Words*) 84
Elegy (I) 85
Elegy (II) 86
Elegy (III) 87
The Jade Incense Burner 88

Downfall Imagined   89
An Attempt at Composing Four Triplets   90
Title Lost (VI)   91
To Jŏng-hi   93
Having Bidden Farewell to Jŏng-hi   94
Title Lost (VII)   95
Title Lost (VIII)   96
A Fragment   97

Index   98
Chronology of the Poet   101
About the Translator   102

Preface

It is a pity that Pak Yong-chŏl (1904–1938) has been underestimated not only as a poet but also as one of those who contributed to opening a new horizon for modern Korean poetry during the dark age when the whole nation was suffering from lack of national pride and futuristic vision for the country. Dying in his mid-thirties, when the whole country was in a state of spiritual torpor and despondency over the apparent non-existence of the possibility of political and social amelioration, he could not harbor any hope for the future either for his own life or for the country.

His life was like a flash of lightning. As I have a glimpse of his brief life, I cannot help comparing it with that of John Keats, who also had such a brief life but attained the zenith's height as a poet. The only difference between the lives of the two is that Keats, despite his personal misfortune of being a victim of the then fatal illness of lung consumption, lived at a time when Romanticism was reaching its height, and he could ride the high-rising tide of that literary movement. Pak Yong-chŏl's life was devastated not only by his health: he spent his thirty-some years' life-span when the whole nation was enwrapped in the gloom of pessimism and despondency, while groaning under the oppression of the colonial rule of the military expansionists of a neighboring country.

The paucity of the remaining poetical works of Pak Yong-chŏl does not mean that he wrote little. While he lived and wrote, he did not even have any desire for fame, 'that last infirmity of noble mind,' and didn't care to have his writings regularly published during his lifetime. It was only after his death that the publisher of *Shi-mun-hak*, a poetry journal he helped to create in 1930 and contributed to in his lifetime, published *The Collected Writings of Pak Yong-chŏl* in three volumes. But even this collection of his writings does not contain all the poems he may have written. More than half of the collection is occupied by his Korean translations from Goethe, Heine, Rilke, Shakespeare, and Ibsen. At a time when Korean literary scene was being contaminated by several ideology-mongers, Pak Yong-chŏl remained a pure man of letters, who was content to live and die with an ardor for the essential beauty of poesy flowing from Parnassus, not for the fame on printed pages. His name was indeed writ in ink, not to be locked up in bound volumes.

Sung-Il Lee
April 24, 2024

A Thank-you Note

I thank Professor Robert Bjork, of Arizona State University, Professor John Hill, formerly of The U.S. Naval Academy, Dr. Danna Messer, of Arc Humanities Press, and Mr. Stanley Barkan, poet and publisher of Cross-Cultural Communications, for providing critique on this book.

Professor Kyung Hwan Moon, a former colleague of mine at Yonsei University, read my manuscript upon my request. He responded to it with the eyes of a reader unfamiliar with the original poems, thereby making me reconsider my translation of a number of lines. (SL)

Poems

A Boat Ready to Set Sail

I, too, am leaving.
Should I waste my youth,
Only shedding tears?
I, too, am leaving.

Will it be easy to leave this snug harbor behind?
It gleams to my eyes glazed, as if befogged.
The folks I loved, whose wrinkled faces are
As familiar as the hills in every dale I've visited!

As the one about to leave is unable to forget,
How can he be different from one chased off?
The clouds I turn to look on are flurried by wind.
Will there be a hillock where I can moor?

I, too, am leaving.
Should I waste my youth,
Only shedding tears?
I, too, am leaving.

After Sending You off on a Night Train

A lone candle flame flickering to fade away
    Into stark darkness!
My aching heart I try to soothe after sending
    You off in this snowstorm!
Feeling sore and hollow, my heart welcomes
    The snowflakes sweeping on it,
While each step of mine ready to slip and fail,
    Leaving its trace on the snow,
Is like one I have to carry on endlessly.

You, who are trying to look out of the window,
    Must be feeling sorrowful;
Your eyes seeing only the reflection of your face
    On the dark window must be full of tears.
When I enter my room, your eyes hiding
    At every nook of it will beam at me;
My skin will feel the tender stroke
    Of your voice and eyes that linger there.
Having sent you away, I feel only desolate.

You, going through darkness like an icebreaker
    Voyaging on a frozen sea—
You, who, having shaken off tender feelings,
    Are on your way to brightness—
Will you be surprised, even if you are shattered,
    While rushing on the two rails?
Will you fear death, while you dash, rolling
    On the track charged with vigor?
Carrying yourself, being carried, you only get far.

If bleak winter is here now, let me wait
    For the spring that will not be far off.
Let me wait for the train you'll ride back,
    That will rush in, beaming like spring.

Can I utter the word 'forget'? Let me learn
   To smile, whatever pain I may feel.
While so doing, let me learn how to follow
   Your steps you carry on the rough road.
Eventually I may be one following your steps.

Though Unable to Go Away Like This

Though I may not take my leave like this,
And may not say no, if I must leave like this,

Like a petal quietly wilting in the windless air,
Like a patch of cloud fading into the blue sky,

If a little bit of fever stops the slow flow of blood,
And my feeble breath has to fade away now—
Ah, beneath the window that lets in faint light,
Tears, uncontrollable, flow to drench my chest.

Chilled Forehead

When I sit alone with a bright light on in immense darkness,
Loneliness surges to make me feel as if I were deprived of all.
If I had a wild flower nearby, what solace would it give to me!

As my eyelids fall down, as if I were being deprived of all,
My whole body turns into a glittering lump of phosphorescence.
What a joy would it be, had I but the company of a dark cricket!

When I burn up my body in the blue gleam, my chilled forehead
Clears up, and it finally enables me to feel the tickling of nerve.
Had I but a star to cherish, what a joyful company would it be!

Home

What's the point of seeking my old home now?
Away from the crumbling hut my family has scattered.
An evening crow must be cawing over autumn grass;
The brook before the village must've changed its flow.

Having left my childhood dreams on my mother's grave,
I have drifted along with the wandering clouds, blown on
By the wind, ready to stop any minute, for over ten years;
For what purpose should I seek my old home now?

Should I draw a new joyful picture on the rim of the sky?
Did I leave anything behind that I am unable to forget?
You, harsh wind, blow on, as hard as you may wish to.
Where can the scattered petals find repose while drifting?

The thought of my home savagely trodden by brutal feet
—Though I often rush to it in my mesmerizing dreams—
Comes back alive like a bitter memory of old love,
As I recall our resolutions robbed off by other people.

Whereto?

Whereto should I let my mind rush?
Dreary rain keeps falling ceaselessly,
And the painful memory of the past
Looms, covering me like dark clouds.

My new-sprung hope I had long given up—
Thought of you that I had wished to erase—
Comes back, flashing in the dark, like lightning.
Yet you are up there so high where I can't reach.

Ah, whereto should I turn my mind for peace?

Rain

Rain falls down and down in endless streaks,
Falls without stopping to rest, falls for no reason,
Drenching the trees and the roofs helplessly stuck.
The whistle of the upward train is heard from nearby;
The train completely wet with rain must look pitiful.
From my heart, too, an eerie thing crawls out, shaking.

Rain falls down and down in endless streaks,
And I feel like rushing to you, like a chicken entirely drenched.
I feel like slithering toward you like a snake across a stream.
A swallow with blackish-red feathers would glide in the air;
But my heart trembles more than a leaf glittering rain-soaked,
Endlessly circling around your room lightened bright.

To whom am I writing to unpack this imploration of mine?
On such a day, if a full-grown girl drowns in a river, no trace will be left,
For, either before or after, only raindrops will hit the surface of the water.
As the rain is not the tear someone has shed, there's nothing sad about it.
But wherefore does the wayfarer leave his footsteps behind welling?
The causeless rain, whether harboring a thought or not, keeps falling.

The Fairy's Song
—Shed no tear—O shed no tear!
   The flower will bloom another year. (Keats)

Waving my wings slowly, I float in the air.
The endless stream flows down on and on.

Young one, do not allow your heart to beat so much, thinking
The bright window over there drawn with a blue curtain
Is half-open, because it is waiting for you.
Slowly waving my wings, I float about in midair.

Young one, do not let your heart fret, imagining
The bright eyes clear as a lake where the moon is immersed
Send a sweet smile to you, casting an amorous glance on you,
While the running brook flows down endlessly.

It is not for your sake, my dear.
Don't presume to think that a mesmerizing
Peony blossoms bloom to please only your eyes.
A butterfly fluttering by entered its bosom unawares;
And slowly waving my wings, I float on in the air.

Don't presume that the titmice among the pine leaves
Sing their songs of jubilee only to please your ears.
Two of them met, and crossing their feathers, flew to that vale,
While the running brook flows down without stopping.

Do know, my dear child, all this is not for your sake.
The running brook flows down without stopping.

Ah, if you have known this, have understood all this,
Then lift your head. A tear-washed face—
Just like a face emerging from deep water—
Will solemnly shine with a light heretofore unseen.
My dear child, learn how to live, enduring loneliness.

Waving my wings slowly, I float in the air.
The endless stream flows down on and on.

Words of a Maiden Leaving for a Far-off Place*

Now I am leaving.
Not letting a stream of tear flow down, I am leaving.

Mother, don't cover your eyes with your skirt hem.
All of you, too, fare well.
In the dim light of the dawn your faces look unfamiliar;
Let me reassure your look once again.
Don't make a fuss for no reason,
For my mind might falter and change.

You, red hills, and green grass, fare you well.
You, brooks gurgling over the pebbles, flow on, frolicking.
—Am I leaving once and for all? Why such a long farewell!
Touch-me-not, didn't you dye my fingernails till last year?

Soon-i, Gŭm-i, Nam-i, my friends of our shiny days!
Now I may have no one nearby I may call a 'friend'!
Let me touch your long braided hair once again.

The red ribbons binding your hair flashing over the fences!
Your laughter rolling down you had no will to stop!
That it all has become a tale to tell, as if others'!
That I now look back, and miss the days
When I grew up as a girl blooming like a lily
In the bliss of absolute purity and being carefree!

What need for shedding tears?
I have to leave anyway. As my departure is not final,
Till we meet again, please remain the way you are now.

---

*In olden days, in Korea, most marriages were arranged by the parents, who were helped by the matchmakers. In many cases, the bride and the bridegroom had their first encounter at the marriage ceremony. Moreover, for a bride-to-be, 'going to her husband's home'—the literal translation of the Korean phrase, '시집가다'—meant an almost lifelong separation from her parents. Nowadays, the tearful leave-taking described in the poem will be hard to understand.

Father, what road is this I've to get on?
Why is it that, shedding tears, we have to bid farewell?
Are the dry leaves bound to be blown off by the wind?
Is a new life possible only when one bids farewell
To what one is familiar with to get drifted on a wide sea?

Swallowing all my endless worries and futile complaints,
I am taking my leave now, while I rub my face
With the two hands of mine that have turned cold.

A Little Devil

My heart is now like coal tar boiling up
In a kettle, while emanating unbearable stench.

The gurgling of the nearby rivulet sounds irksome,
And the frogs' croaking causes unbearable annoyance.
Recalling the thatched roof of the stuffy hut
I am forced to stoop low to enter, I turn back
Ten times, and wielding a stick like a sword,
I beat the guiltless branches and leaves.

Even the sneering stars have hidden, while
The crescent half moon wrapped in clouds is dim.
Languid drowsiness rules over the whole land, while
Hunger forces fingernails to scratch panels desperately.

In the dreary rain fungus prospers on noble sentiments,
And flaunting around on the back of foolishness luckily found,
Dwarfs roll, thinking that it is a masterful skill;
Then, a bunch of asses laugh, opening their idiotic mouths.

How can I more carry on this vituperation?
Now my feelings have turned into pieces of paper
Crumpled and torn to be thrown away as rubbish.

Lines from 'The Soft Wings'

In vain you flap your soft wings,
    For the blue sky can never be reached,
    And the road in your dream runs faintly.
You flap your soft wings feebly.

        *

Whereto does this road lead?
On whose feet do those clouds cross the hill?
The sun about to set is hung over the hill, and
Only the homeless birds flock, filling the sky.

        *

A day, indeed, is like another day: wherefore
Should a certain day be an unforgettable one?

When two mirrors face each other,
Endless mirroring occurs on them;
    Where will this mirroring end?

Like a dog barking in fear of none that is,
You at times bark with full throat; but,
What is it that you are waiting for?

Of the pupils ordered to line up in close array,
Which one is the sad son of mine?
Rain falls ceaselessly and with no sign of stopping.
Upon the pavement veneered with reflecting water
He walks—with collar raised and thoroughly soaked—
Nonchalantly and with full composure, despite
The hovel he has to seek, the gate he'll have to enter
With his head lowered, and the room with no sign of heating—
He simply keeps on walking around.

*

All of a sudden, his heart blooms like a flower;
Then, soon he lowers his head again, feeling ashamed.
He feels his blood resuming its flow in happiness;
Then, anxiety makes his heart beat again.

You, who carry rapid steps, with collar unfolded!
To which house on the slope over there are you returning?
Tell me, bird,
Are you, too, returning to a friend waiting for you?
Now,
In the shade of each tree branch,
From the center of its dimness looms a new face.

*

Is it what you are telling me?
That I should love all this?
How on earth
Can I love all this?
Haven't you noticed that I've ever
Loved what is beautiful?
But, look,
Where is that beauty that makes my heart leap up?
    Blue sky and the frequent sunshine,
    And the beautifully-curving hills and streams,
    And the trees and the flowers—
    Do not say anymore.
    What did they add to augment beauty?
    What did they create?

No Title

Ah, but,
'Home'! 'Home'!
In this word lurks a supreme command.
Like a baby struggling to be freed from strong arms,
My heart is about to split into two parts.
Dear friend, teach me how
I can be freed from loving this hometown of mine.

   "Walk around with your eyes closed.
   Walk around with your ears clogged.
   Otherwise, leave this place once and for all."

Hope and Despair

What sun or moon has such strong magnetism?
The tide surging unto my heart over and again!

The swelling watery surface rises like oil,
And a few seagulls cross their flights in midair,

While the sails full-blown by the wind
Get ready to embark on a far-reaching voyage.

But as a patch of cloud fleets by at the moment,
My heart sinks, and its flag-pole gets broken.

The rugged rocks reveal their hidden faces again,
And the black mud has ceased to beckon death.

The fishes flopping in the remaining water-pools,
And the seaweeds that have cast themselves hastily—

When chance has not been entangled like hair,
Why are you casting a fishing rod in vain hopes?

Hovering between the two hills of hope and despair,
I waver like the pendulum of a clock to and fro.

What a dizzying game of hide and seek so foolish
That cannot be caught up by the rapid wings of poesy!

This futile movement of breathing in and out—
Do you gasp short of breath, more than a cow in June?

Rainy Day

While rain falls constantly all day long,
My heart starts pining away at long last.
The guiltless gulls may've died, all wet.

From Despair

Now I'm a seed buried and crouching
Prostrate in the mud of despair.
   Ah, this boundless
   Darkness and quietude!
However, however,
   Slowly, very slowly,
I lift my head,
   Slowly, very slowly,
   But not yet daunted.
I push my head upward. . . .
I breathe, and pierce through the Earth—
   I stretch out my arms—
   I stretch out my legs—
Ah, now I am a man standing
On a hill shone by the morning sun,
With my two arms spread wide.

Be Nobler!
—He fears lest his love should fall.

Ascend higher and higher, till no one can reach you.
Shine serenely where the blue sky stretches far above.
    Your face looms in the clear water welling in my heart;
    Proud am I to have a longing for you as cold as a star.

But the fear I feel deep in my trembling heart—
    Entrusting hyacinths on the hillock to a shepherd's feet, I fear
    Lest I make the clear well turn muddy with the stone I throw—
Oh, what if this eternal mirror gets shattered to pieces!

Ascend higher and higher, till no one can reach you;
I shall be proud to long for you with star-like coldness.

The Horse I Loved

The horse I once lovingly stroked is now before my eyes.
His once lustrous hair, his snowy whites, his sinewy hind legs,
The audacity of his posture! None of these remains to be seen.
Yet my deep-seated love for him enables me to recognize him.

This shabby, worn-out horse pulling a cart, bearing a harness,
Was once the beautiful creature I was so much enamored of,
The pony that, in the spring sunlight pouring on a wide grassy field,
Would run on its four hooves, neighing loudly, and then gallop lightly.

With no dot of a will to raise his eyes to look up on the sky,
Exhausted of the last drop of energy to jump up two feet high,
Driven around by the whip incessantly falling on his haunch,
He lowers his head to eat the fodder in a manger hung on his neck.

Watching him with an aching heart and two fists trembling in anger,
I can neither close my eyes, nor turn them up to the deep, lofty sky.

As I'm Not Yours

As I'm not yours, I haven't faded in you.
    Yet, though I truly wish I haven't faded,
Just as candlelight fades in bright daylight,
    Just as snowflakes fade away on the sea,

So I still love you. In my eyes, you are still
    A person beautiful and emanating light.
    I can still see your beauty and radiance.

But though I wish to remain the way I am—
    To fade away the way light does in rain—

Oh, throw me into the deep bosom of love.
    Pull all my senses to deafen and blind me,
The way your love, swept by a snowstorm,
    Flickers like a candle flame in the wind.

An Owl is Hooting

      I

An owl is hooting.
An owl is hooting.
In the deep, windy, cloudy night,
An owl is hooting.
In the dark where snow melts down like taffy,
An owl is hooting.
A lone hut in the middle of darkness—
A faint light comes out of its window.
An owl is hooting, while the light flickers.
An owl is hooting, when the light fades out.

      II

An owl is hooting.
An owl is hooting.
Wet with dew, pitiful grass falls to lie down,
And an owl is hooting.
From the dark earth rises a strange shadow,
And an owl is hooting.
A wolf wandering about a grave,
Drawing out its tail, lowers its head.
An owl is hooting, while the light flickers.
An owl is hooting, when the light fades out.

      III

An owl is hooting.
Is it a hooting calling for something?
What are you trying to call out for?
An owl is hooting.
An owl is hooting.
The blood-stained ghost with hair disheveled
That appears in every ghost story—
An owl is hooting,
An owl is hooting.

Like a ghost stretching its height,
Between the clouds and the earth,
Wind blows, whistling and rushing.
An owl is hooting, while the light flickers.
An owl is hooting, when the light fades off.
Oh, the light has completely gone out.
An owl is hooting.
An owl is hooting.
. . . .

A Grave and the Moon

As the soul remains, though a body is gone,
So a stream of thought continues to flow.

   Let the bluish-pale moonbeam
   Shine, falling on my body,
   Let it shine the whole night.
   On my cheeks hollowed after long illness,
   On my chilled body with the stain of blood,
   Let the pale moonbeam
   Fall plenteously.

Where the dark shadow of pines lingers,
Upon the grass bearing the pale moonbeam,
A stream of thought continues to flow.
While the pale moon sheds silvery threads,
Even the entangled thoughts melt down,
And like haze throwing white shadow,
Fade away, leaving no trace.

A Heart Soaked with Rain

Collapsing on the floor of a cold and dark room,
He breathes out a deep sigh, uttering, "Ah, Mother!"
All the sorrows he has swallowed with clenched teeth
Pour out from his chest along with this single word,
The way a carefully-built tower crumbles down.

Having foundered through much sneer and contempt,
He has no vigor to raise his body worn as old cotton,
And only darkness and gloom fill up his mind and heart,
As he sits in his room with no warmth of a company,
While the night wears on with the cold rain drizzling.

Having found solace in the single word he uttered unawares,
Just like a child crying, holding a hem of his mother's cloth,
After being harassed by the mischievous kids of the village,
He, feeling the tender touch of his mother's consoling hand,
Weeps on to his heart's content to be purged of all his pain.

A Fragment of Thought (I)

Occasionally, though not so often,
I find living not so savory.
Even so,
No need to decide to die willfully.
Therefore,
I keep limping on, dragging one leg.

While living on, forgetful of being alive,
I look back to find it meaningless.
No need to live on purposefully—
Nevertheless,
Not so easy to give up life willfully.
Our laughter sounds hollow,
And 'joy' is a word to disappear from lexicon.

I have made up my mind to remain a pessimist.

A Fragment of Thought (II)

That one must gladly embrace pain and grief
Is an injunction the wise men have imposed on us.
But I live on, swallowing all, as if I were being avenged.
Certain days come when I don't feel like living on.
Those days are more precious than when I live mindless.
I feel envious of the birds that don't have to work for living.
Is it an ordinary happening that one is given birth?
Had I known I'd live like this, I'd have died long ago.

Title Lost (I)

Pygmy poet! How dare you come and stand before me!
What words are you planning to gabble before me?
Watching me shed tears, unable to suppress longing
For an endlessly wide open field of Africa
With shady dense woods and loudly pouring streams,
Do you intend to draw my face as that of a 'poet,' who,
With a lank and lean face, weeps over losing a wench?
Throw away that sugary stuff that you call 'sorrow,'
And take what boils in my heart into yours, so that
You may claim my words of magnitude as yours, 'poet'!

Title Lost (II)

You laugh at me.
Upon hearing me say,
"Now I want to live a life,"
You laugh at this big resolution of mine,
With a laughter
Ringing clear like a bell, implying:
"Is there anything new?"

Upon hearing that I've not lived a life,
You laugh loudly, unable to suppress guffaw.
When I said, "Life's but a walking shadow,"
You sneered at me unabatedly,
The way sunbeams spread wide.

"Lest the day comes when you know it,
I cannot but fear."

Winter Solstice

I turn my eyes to the North
Only to see white clouds enter it
Through the dry tree branches,
From which leaves have fallen off.

As I lie pleasantly inebriated,
I cannot tell day from night;
What significance to realize
That it is the winter solstice?

Oblivion

Ah, beautiful oblivion!

Were it not for you, even God
Is only a helpless elementary school kid!
Paper bearing poor brush strokes should be
Crumpled and thrown away into a trash bin.

Every dawn the water-seller leans
His squeaking shoulder-pole to pour water
Into the tilting dried-up crock pot till it gets full.
Whose hand
Is it that with delicate fingers
Carefully winds up a watch?

What a tender job it is
To wipe away what's written on a blackboard!
The strange smile on the face of a blind man,
Who, groping on the trace of your eraser,
Can read what were written there!

Day and night
A short-track runner repeats
Practice of making a start.
Ah, life is jolly.

A Love-song

Do you call this a manifestation of sheer stupidity?
Now the flame of my life has gradually subsided,
So that desire for the world evaporates like fume,
I'd rather seek my beloved to say a word to her?

Holding her hand with both of mine upon my breast,
Or, if not, perusing her face in silence,
Or, if not, lowering my face with my eyes downcast,
I may say to her: "Please forgive me, dear."

Was it not an argument on a trifle?
Was it not a vainglorious self-aggrandizing?
Each turning away from our shared home,
We blocked our way for returning!

In many a dream, without hesitation,
I have knelt down before your feet.
Ah, tell me whether you, too,
Have done so, haven't you?

Though you vaunt in your flashing garment,
And keep a smiley face as you walk,
I know that darkness reigns in your heart.
I know it, have seen it.

All the knots of grievance and discontent
Have been unraveled, each of them,
And just as the setting sun dyes a field in pink,
Regret and repentance settle on me.

Just as the piled-up snow may be swept off,
Your frozen heart may melt down to flow on.
So, please, dear, release your love closed in,
And come to me, afloat on the sea of pardon.

Holding my hands together, I gaze on you,
With no words to utter other than "Forgive me."
When our two hearts reunited melt down together,
I may head to the land of eternal peace and sweet sleep.

Sentimental

                I

In the azure sky sunlight reasserts itself,
And silvery clouds glitter like fish fins,
Urging, "Let's go ahead! Let's go ahead!"
Go? Whereto are you telling me to go?

Beneath a pine tree I stop walking.
I stroll to a grassy spot only to fall on my bottom.
Ah, my heart is already stuffy and aches enough;
Why do you poke into it to make it feel worse?

Are you calling me out to stroll to where
The tune of a violin is sobbing on an autumn day?
Upon a road where I do not know what to look for,
Why tell me to walk, gasping with a gushing desire?

                II

Upon that wide field stirs a yellowish energy,
And over the apple yard red lights get entangled.
Mounts arrayed like a folding screen receive me politely,
And a thoroughfare stretches itself, not showing its end.

Ah, under this fair sky, within this fine air,
I cannot indulge in uninhibited drunkenness,
Reverently holding a cup overflowing with the sunlight
Ripening fruits, nor sink deep like a sea in gratification.

Unable to suppress tears drowning me all over,
I remain immobile and spellbound, while I dare not stir.

Renewed Happiness

When the bluish black night has descended
To cover the whole world with its sacred spirit,
Let love haunting around you day and night
Steal away from your sight
And lie down alone on the hill over there.
After watching the starry sky nonchalantly,
Let it close its eyes in languor.
Then, a brighter world will be revealed to mind's eye,
While happiness begins to stir up like wave,
And the good thoughts of regret and forgiveness
Spurt like fishes frolicking in a stream.
At such a moment, far over there,
Along the slope of the mounts soaring dark,
A torch-light will fleet, as if in flight,
Toward home that should be brightened.
Bearing fear and longing intermingled,
You, too, will hasten back on the dark road
To enter the hut a comforting light brightens.
The eyes cast on you when you arrive will
Make you feel as if a long separation were ended,
And with renewed happiness will greet you.

Shiny Trace

As the warm bright sunlight flows down like this,
The long-hidden sprouts come out, whispering,
And the pink petals on the new-sprung shy branches
Never try to refuse the kisses poured down on them.

Where blue moonbeams shine, dewdrops turn into bijoux,
And even water welling on a road, like a lake, lets in stars.
The small fireflies, though mere insects of a summer night,
Are the comets fleeting by, trailing light from their tails.

Ah, my dear, throw away demeaning love that forces you
To kneel to beg for love of a wench with a slender waist;
Turn into a man that emanates inborn light from his body.

Leave 'love' that makes you droop with a trembling heart!
Soar high like a silvery dove with your chest pushed forward,
So, though with dim eyes, let me follow your shining flight!

I Commit Him to the Flame

At last I commit him to the flame—
The one who owns all I love and cherish.
Will a handful of ash be left? I burn him.

As the sooty, rough earth is not right for him,
I only let the white smoke rise up high and far.

Even the sky is not blue, but is of ashen gray,
And not even a single lively brook flows on
In the wrinkle of a valley dark, red and yellow;
But the wind that has been hiding in bare branches
Blows on the white smoke, making it swirl and scatter.
Having lost a dear one going away farther than eternity,
Should I look for gold in the ashes, as if an alchemist?

Ah, the feeling of willfully shattering a precious jewel!
The feeling of burying in the mud the most precious incense!
Swallowing the bitter juice oozing from the gall I chew,
I sit on a rugged rock, not caring where my body is thrown.

Two Birds

—Two birds perched side by side with gray in the background:
　Each of the two birds has turned its back to the world.
　　One of them has an ailing heart, the other an aching chest.

"Sister, does your heart beat as a fish leaps in a dry stream?
Or, is it about to crumble to pieces like dried-up leaves?
Or, is it like an empty spindle turning on an oil-dry axle?
Ah, pitiful! Yet, despite your own illness, you worry that
Your brother's face is not ruddy enough, but yellowish, and
He spits out the red petals of a camellia blooming in his chest.
Ah, as our hands meet, yours is as cold as a white candle stick.

"We were born in this land of dry earth, beneath this low-lying roof.
Though we have been living after sending all our joy to the sky's edge,
We stoop to flatter, hoping to live in a house draped with silk curtains.

"They say a dying swan flaps a pair of eye-dazzling wings.
With our shabby wings, we look pitiful like rain-soaked chicks.

"We are two ailing chicks that have lost both dad and mom.
What wind is blowing, making these branches tremble so much?"

Again

Sitting amidst the rugged rocks near a rivulet
That has dried up and stopped warbling,
I watch the murky sky,
I watch the naked branches,
I watch the smoke rising.

Even the word *nada* sounds hollow.

Dear childlike heart,
Tender heart,
You, too,
Dry up like this,
And crouching,
Turn into a rock rugged as this.

Having brooked the pain of burning you,
What else can I not put into flame?

*Satyrs**

Indeed, we've become impossible to wash and iron,
For, once stained with splashed mud or machine oil,
There's nothing you can do about it.
It is a pity, indeed.
Since starching or beating is impossible,
And it is hard to rinse us in flowing water,
What about letting us fall like planes shattered in midair!
Washed clothes hung upside down to get dried,
While flapping in the wind, are to be envied much.
Every valley is reverberating with the sound
Our mothers make while beating the clothes.

---

* In this poem, the word "Satyrs" is a metaphor for the kids irredeemably spoiled. All the mothers' agony over their children, whom they think irretrievably lost, is metaphorically referred to by their act of beating the wrinkled clothes spread on the stone block with the round wooden sticks.

A Jolly Night

Has ever November in Seoul been as tender as this?
Has ever the air on Jong-ro Street been so fresh as to broaden our chests?
"Ha, ha, ha," laughter loosens wrinkles, and the sky steps back, alarmed.

From a taxicab crawling, as if gliding, under the electric light,
Two of us, dear to each other, look out;
And, as a little one carrying his steps in a hurry fleets by,
Our queen raises her reddish-brown coat collar over her black muffler.

—"That pork cutlet was so smeared with gravy that it was almost like soup."
—"Yet that girl's mouth looked so pretty."
(Her hair, not covered even with a borrowed cap, floated around freely.)

Our escort, take a route for us to go by the most roundabout way.
As our footsteps on the asphalt pavement are too light,
What if the road branches into three? No way to turn back!

Those well-dressed chaps chuckling over nothing may fall into dancing soon.

As my skin feels sore and numb, as if it had been anointed with balm,
The hot coffee poured in my empty stomach must've been brewed from my blood!

Good night, have a nice dream. Knock at the door to make it sound.
Now, then, let's shake hands, and part here, to the east, to the west.
Ouch! I almost hit the shoulder of the one walking ahead of me. . . .

Title Lost (III)

Where on earth is it guaranteed that tomorrow morning the sun is bound to rise again in the eastern sky? Are we supposed to believe so?

Where is the dog that will bite the moon to bring it here, the hound that will bite the sun to bring it here, to this land as dark as in a tale?

Title Lost (IV)

The moon over there is waning again;
    Grown full round, it wanes again.
As frost-bearing clouds loom above,
    Leaves rustle, knowing what's ahead.
September, October, and then November—
    September, October, and then November—
As I follow the fleeting of the months,
    Unbidden tears well in my eyes.

Chrysanthemum— should we call it a flower?
    As it doesn't bear any fruit,
    As no butterflies fly unto it,
    Only the scent of cold wind digs deep into it.
Having spent summer's day with its young body lying,
    It blooms far less red than the autumn leaves,
    While crickets chirp louder than the birds in spring.

Snow Falls

On this winter morning
Snow falls.

As the snow is so white,
And as its falling sounds so suppressed,

I feel like lowering my head to pray.

My dear, now a tinge of sorrow
Settles on your lips to dye them,

Do you, too, love this snowfall?

Now snow is falling,
It is time for us to pray together.

Upon the Sand on a Moonlit Night

While strolling on the sand rustling under my feet,
On the beach where the reeds shed their silent shadows,
I saw, ah, on the white sand, a green frog lying supine,
With its swollen white belly fully exposed.
Upon seeing it, instantaneously I smelt
That indescribable, yet revealing, smell of death!

I turned my grief-stricken forehead to the sky;
And, as if to hear the whisper of the blue moon,
I stopped walking to stand on the sand in silence.

Snow (I)

Let's walk, let's keep on walking,
Treading the snow newly fallen.
On the snow we leave our footsteps.
Dear Soon, let's walk on the snow.

Snow's hug is warmer than people's world.
Dear Soon, let's walk on, treading the snow.

In front of us fresh snow is falling endlessly.
Behind us a new lane appears, following us.
Dear Soon, let's keep walking on the snow.

Our walking is upward on a slope;
After three steps forward, we slide back.
Only after ten steps, we manage to get forward.

Your clothes and skin are as white as snow;
Your hair is as dark as a wood of pine trees.
In the midst of this, I may lose the trace of you.
Dear Soon, let's keep walking on the snow.

With our bodies and hearts made as pure as snow,
Let us fly up lightly and joyfully like the snow.
Dear Soon, let's fly over the snow lightly, airily.

A Certain Night

In the evening the frogs croaked;
Finally, as night comes, rain falls.

On my yard even drearier in the summer,
Rain falls with a sound suppressed.

But then, what is happening now? From somewhere
The sound of an insect chirping comes, intermittently.

Just like a frog that has stopped croaking now,
My heart remains boundlessly calm and tranquil.

Night

You, my mind, be of more magnitude!
For you only try in vain. . . .
Ah, is it not in truth futile and hollow?

The foolish leaves of grass in the south
Lift their faces up to the sunbeam of a deceptive winter day,

Hoping to see a patch of cloud drifting in the droughty sky,
Like a searing tree branch that spreads its arms wide.

You, a strange wayfarer, carrying on a night journey,
Vainly allow your hope to spread its wings—the way
A candle flame faintly glimmers to brighten a lone hillside hut.

With that thin string of wisdom strangle and slice the neck of hope.

Keep walking, carrying your heavy load, while dragging your wearied legs.
Keep walking on the road, though you don't know whereto you are bound.
Keep walking, still embracing the flameless charred wood in your bosom.
Keep walking into the night whereto dawn will not come back.

The Kite and the Blue Pool

            I

The clear blue sky is infinitely lofty,
And the swarming ants remain only diligent.
As the broad-winged kite sweeps down,
A clan of chickens hides under the fence.

My eyes big and round in bewilderment
Finally are forced to be turned away.
"What's the point of being here?"
My thoughts only sink down into despair.

           II

The blue pool underneath a black rock
Swallows up all the shadows cast on it.
Yet a darkish bird sitting on a branch's tip
Is still singing, watching its shadow.

As that bird large and broad looms like a canopy,
I am caught in its inescapable grip; yet only by
Clenching my teeth tightly, I may somehow expel it.
If I slacken my breath, its grip may even reach my chest.

As I shudder all over with my eyes closed,
My arms I stretch to wave feel entangled;
My hair disheveled in the swirl of the blue pool
Grips me, and pulls me down into despair.

A Song of the Listless Wind

I am only a gust of wind
Blowing, unaware of
All the joy the world yields.
I am a mindless gust of wind
That blows, for no reason,
On the butterflies and the petals,
On a pair of lips
Sending out whispers,
Inaudible as they are.

I am only a gust of wind
Blowing, unaware of
All the joy the world yields.
While those stooping over the earth
Shed sweat on their backs,
While the steel-hardening hammers
Are lifted high and fall down hard,
I remain a gust of wind
That passes by nonchalantly.

I am only a gust of wind
Blowing, unaware of
All the joy the world yields.
Where yellowed ears
Lower their heads uniformly,
Where red apples
Ripen to adorn the foot of a hill,
I remain a gust of wind blowing
Like a sigh, earning no profit.

I am only a gust of wind
Blowing, unaware of
All the joy the world yields.
When the boughs shorn of leaves

Tremble, weeping silently,
And when a black crow caws
To erase the sun setting down,
I walk away, leaving no trace,
As I blow on without any feeling.

Finding nothing in this world
That draws my heart,
I rise up by myself,
Finally to fade away;
I am a gust of wind
That blows, attaining no joy.

Title Lost (V)

    Lightly flow the words borne on the smile we exchange. Yet, look, my eyes are wet with tears. I feel that indescribable sadness is billowing over me.

    Yes, yes, we know that we can tell jokes, and, oh, yes, we know that we also can smile silently. Yet, within this heart of mine, there is something—I don't know what that is—that neither your words lightly said can put to rest, nor your laughter of joy can calm.

    Give me your hand, and, let all sound cease to be heard. Turn the crystal-clear eyes of yours to me, my beloved, so that I may read your innermost thought therein.

    Ah! Is even love so languid that it can't release innermost thoughts to be uttered? Even between two of us, who are in love, do we find it too hard to release the true thoughts to each other? Have we become so weakened? I have always known that people tend to hide their innermost thoughts for fear that others may take them as lightly as a passing wind, or find fault with them.

A Fracture of the Sky

I lift my eyes by chance to look out of the window;
Then a fracture of the blue sky comes into my view.

Recalling how long I have been forgetful of the sky,
I feel glad, as if something lost had been retrieved.

Though confined in a small room of four walls,
My heart leaps, as if I were standing on a hill overlooking
A wide-open field, bearing the sky like a round canopy,
While stroking a rock; so full of joy is my heart!

Small Sky

To my sky,
Even to this sky of mine so small,
Birds come, flying in.

To this sky no wider than the gap
Between the upper eave and the lower eave,
Birds with slender bodies come, flying in.

Having flown here by chance,
Soon they fly away.
Shadows that fade away,
Shadows that fade away,
Shadows fading away, leaving no trace,
Are all shadows fading away empty nothing?

Birds fly away in leisure.

Your Shadow

White sand
Stretches boundlessly;

Above a patch of cloud
A song has hidden.

Your shadow
Lingering like haze,

With longing,
Is pining away all alone.

A Chance Encounter

He stopped with eyes wide-open,
Like a clock suddenly out of order.

A Clock That Has Stopped

I have never thought
You'd make such a solemn face.

A Doll

Please look at me.
Look at me, please.

Please touch me a little.
Don't your fingertips feel thrilled?

Why no one composes a poem,
As a poet did for Beatrice?

Mademoiselle Typist

What trickery is this again that a mere machine
Shows fatigue on its face?

If you want to learn how to find the correct letters
The moment an inspiration strikes you,
Please come to me, my dear poet.

Being in Love

That land where, before yesterday is hardly gone,
Another day spreads the ribs of a fan— Ah, aurora!

On the hill flowers bloom exuberantly,
And the numberless birds sing on the boughs.

Snow (II)

When snow falls like a baby toddling around precariously,
I wholeheartedly welcome it.

When snow falls, rustling and spreading its cold touch,
My chilled forehead gets immersed in its lonesome thoughts.

When snow falls, letting its light wear be blown on like petals,
I wonder where within its purity such loose gesture has been hidden.

When a millennium ago I strolled with Sappho on the flowerless hill,
Snow had spread that flawlessly pure, ethereal silk for us to walk on.

Then we walked on it, leaving no trace of our footsteps;
But then, rising above it as vapor does, we flew over it.

When snow spreads on the earth the patterns woven with quietude and light,
No one can reach out to the stars high up in the sky and pick them.

The Night before

My love, please keep on living.
Ah, my dear love—
While keeping guard of you breathing helplessly
Like a tamed lioness, lying on a flashy bed, ah—
Have I ever liked to utter an ominous word?
Nonetheless,
Dear one, just do not die yet.
Isn't this life worth living?
The sky is so infinitely lofty and blue,
From the persimmon tree dangle its red fruits,
And are we not still young?

Sometimes despair, like a lovely mermaid, beckons us—
Small creatures crawling beneath the sky, upon the earth;
Yet should we take it as a sweet call?

My eyes clear as the stars at dawn have not yet been bedimmed.
And your eyes must be as clear as to see this.
As your skin still retains the smoothness of a silk gown,
You won't be able to loosen your grip on this life.

My dear, just don't loosen your grip on this life.
Am I not a patch of cloud to fade away traceless,
Or a rosebud whose petals can scatter in a minute?
When a steel-built ship can be shattered by the waves,
Who can say that this world's waves aren't so ferocious?
Our love reaching to the sky may renew its daily ascension
Till, on top of our infinite love, we may build another floor.
Shan't the days of our love be prolonged even from now?

When our meeting was so late, how can we part easily?
On rainy days, have you not been reluctant to go far from home?
My dear, how has it all come to happen?

Disregarding all we find precious in this world,
Just for the sake of my heart that resembles a flower pinned on a white shirt,
My dear, please live on.
Won't the other world be dark and cold?
Isn't it a cold place where a loving one can't follow, where no shadows are?
My dear, how can you go there?

Though a season for sorrow is not separately allocated,
Didn't you mention the sorrow of autumn, while in the midst of happiness?
If you are not near me,
Chrysanthemums' fragrance will only be bitter,
The moon bright for no reason, an autumn night too long.

The cawing of the wild geese will only be a well of tears.
When winter comes, won't your grave be too cold to lie in?
Though spring is near, as they say, how can we expect
The crystal-clear brook to flow on, waiting for it?

My dear, do not die.
All the lovely nights filled with all my passion,
All my thoughts embroidered with beautiful dreams—
Take all this into your mind,
And live on, my dear, long.
I pray, burning all my flesh where my young blood flows.
Death, will you not lower your head and succumb?

The Vale of Ten-Thousand Waterfalls

In the midst of a million roars
You still maintain quietude of your own.

Though you show not a tinge of
Movement or a smiley face,

You are lulled, as if in a cradle,
By an everlasting melody;

And from your face looms
Smile of unfathomable depth.

With nothing covering you,
You show your inborn shape.

No tinge of a color
Covers you for disguise;

Awakened to see with innermost eyes,
You don't overstep the bound of your vision.

You don't assume any shape,
For your entirety embodies your spirit.

You are tender,
Yet proudly humble.

Prayer

We are a bunch seeking nothing.
What can we say we wish to be granted?
Just only one lesson that will cool our hearts—
Wherein it will be engraved—let us receive from you.

When we are in noisy multitude, we feel giddy with sickness;
Yet we are far from being wise to enjoy solitude in a mount.
Somewhere, neither of the two, where we won't be bothered,
Let us dwell with our hearts that remain calm and peaceful.

Lord, we pray Thee to forgive us.
Forgive us when we fall into laughter without discretion;
Pitying our tears, forgive us when we burst into crying.
Lead us by reaching out to hold our hands,
As we walk into mud in avoidance of the snobs.
Save us from the hands of those trying to redeem the world;
Only nurture us by providing fresh air for us.
When we stagger in drunkenness, nausea, or giddiness,
Rescue us, most of all, from the warmth of people.
Save our days uninhibitedly flat like bald mountains;
When our hands don't know what to do, let them idle away;
When our minds don't obey us like an unwieldy donkey,
Please don't set harness upon us.

From us who don't own anything, take away our grieving hearts,
But let us wait for the morning to come, as a wooden statue does.

Invocation

Winter has deepened long enough. Ah, spring!
How tardy are the steps you carry to be here!
Sun, the stuffy clouds have been there too long!
How rarely you reveal your bright face!

Before the cold and darkness stop our breath,
Please pour fresh blood in our vessels!
We stretch our arms like dry branches to the sky,
And our blank eyes are cast upward in longing.

Like a prince appearing to sit on the throne,
Lifting the heavy-drawn curtain of dreariness,
Show the ruddy, bright face of yours to us
To receive the bowing from us tired of waiting.

Break the clouds impenetrable like a steel kettle's lid,
And grant us to feel your power not to be vanquished.

Our Nursing Mom (The Boy's Words)

The blue sky of liberty is our nursing mom.
We've come in the dark to our nursing mom.
We are young heroes still craving to suck her breast.

      *

The blue sky of liberty is our nursing mom.
Surviving the battles of wielding frosty swords,
We wish to be men bearing the scars on our faces.

      *

The blue sky of liberty is our nursing mom.
Having kicked off the light cotton coverlets unawares,
We finish our youthful dreams upon the cold stones.

Elegy (I)

When I was spending a few months together with you,
The sky was so blue, and overflowed with our laughter;
Yet I never knew then that I'd now call you 'my love.'

Our parting was so abrupt, without any word of leave-taking.
Beneath the sky merging with water, no hope to see you again;
Calling you 'My Love,' I find myself blaming you for my pain.

When we walked on the moonlit sandbar befogged by the haze,
Did we tread on the sand only, carrying our steps hand in hand?
My love, why am I trying to hold a song flowing like a stream?

The summer at a southern isle, where words and insects' chirp mingled—
With my high-pitched voice I shocked the murmuring river.
My dear, I wish you didn't burst into laughter, looking at the sky.

Standing in the yard, I see the moon spreading her boundless beam.
While running together, as if in joy of having our feet freed from tie,
We thought we were the shadows of the sky dancing in jubilee.

Even in a laughter bursting out, the eyes may well with tears;
And if the tears are swallowed, they may make the gall feel sore.
Now I know what we felt on that day, though we said nothing then.

Has the road we trod then with our hearts full of youthful hope
Turned its direction to put us on a road leading to death?
As the gleam of blue beam remains constant, my grief deepens.

Elegy (II)

Though emaciated and cold, you are the same person.
Eyes closed, and breath stopped; do they call it death?
If the journey was so short, can you not reverse it?

Should I talk of grief? Reconsidering, I find it funny.
The hands I touched yesterday have turned into ashes.
Though I know its futility, what shall I do with this grief?

Though smile always lingered around your thick lips,
Teardrops kept rolling from your eyes opaque like bijoux.
Were they morning dews? They faded away so soon.

When I loved you as a friend, depended on you as a brother,
I was like a helpless child, much too often feeling neglected.
Though regret is renewed, how can I have it repaired?

Whenever you saw me, you paid attention to my complexion,
And worried, wondering if I might get plucked off untimely.
Now you went away ahead of me, I wonder if I am in a dream.

When you get there before me, will you find a decent dwelling?
The night when we've settled at a new home, shan't you laugh?
No cause to glee over not having the first visitor to our new home.

Elegy (III)

A millet-stalk fence is raised and the roof thatched anew;
But the alley remains empty and quiet with few entering it.
I'd rather believe that the news I've received is not true.

His frequent scolding came from his deep love for me,
Which hastened his hair turning white much too early.
My heart aches to think I may've precipitated his demise.

Of his five sons, the oldest one is not even twenty;
His daughter living far off is there for mourning.
Hearing their weeping, how could he leave them behind?

He had sent a brother one year ahead. For fifty-three years,
Though of different temper, their brotherly love ever deepened.
Grief over his brother's going away had thickened his wrinkles.

Though of small stature, he emanated dignity, wearing white hair.
He was ever humble, greeting others with his palms put together.
But when he set forth his argument on an issue, he did not yield.

Can anyone be always free from making errors in human affairs?
Can anyone stay away from arguing with others, while living this life?
As he has set out on a long journey, I wish to keep only good memories.

The Jade Incense Burner

I burn the precious incense in the burner in snow-white jade,
While a stream of blue smoke rises to the sky.
My soul, too, seeks the one hidden behind the haze.

While whole-heartedly entrusting my cherished body and soul
To him, extolling his sublime thoughts, with a trembling heart,
I'm ashamed of having conceived him merely as one with a lovely face.

His lofty forehead with transparent skin reveals his wisdom.
May I compare him to a ball of jade looming to dazzle our eyes?
Fondly caressing it, I find it hard to take my palm away from it.

Let the sky smile at me, and let the sun envy me.
Let the stars hide themselves, like shy maidens.
My two arms, embracing my beloved, overflow with joy.

I laugh at the whole world, realizing my heart has been impoverished.
Lifting my heels, I try to jump up, shouting. How free my heart feels!
World, look up at me, for I am a beneficiary of the love of my Lord!

As I inhale the vapor rising from the earth, my heart overflows with green.
The green light shines, as if newly washed, and grows thicker.
Let me hug it as if in madness, and let me rub my cheek on it!

Downfall Imagined

Leaning over forty degrees at the edge of a cliff—
With no other choice, I fall down headlong.
Love, fly up, bearing me upon your wings!

The tall water gate that blocked suddenly disappears,
And my feelings pour down into a bottomless chasm.
When will it be that your love becomes even with mine?

An Attempt at Composing Four Triplets

To say that a spring day is jolly— what a flat lie!
Birdsongs from the wood only augment sadness.
As my love is only one, where else should I cling?

*

I thought my heart could be strong, away from my love;
But once I'm away from my love, what is left of me?
Having given my life to my love, I'll let it prosper there.

*

Hearing the sounds of rain, of leaves, of wind, of birds,
Can I ever be free from the thoughts of my beloved away?
Longing to see my love in a dream, can I forget in waking life?

*

Do they say the mountains are far off, the rivers deep?
When one can make the journey in a dream overnight,
I regret I don't make up my mind to take off right away.

Title Lost (VI)

Though you are boastful of having never strewn tears,
Though you are praised for your unusual fortitude,
Who will blame you for losing composure to wet your eyes?

If you say it's funny, won't saying so sound funny, too?
If you are to surrender to sorrow, won't it be a bit too early?
What to do with tear oozing with smile before sudden fear?

What though I remain calm in the presence of this predicament?
Sister, push off that worry. Wife, wipe off your tears, for now.
Let me write to a few far off, so they may be relieved of worries.

Friend, how can one stain one's lips with the word 'death'!
Though I haven't perused into that affair thoroughly enough,
Whenever the word 'death' rings in my ears, I feel giddy.

Have you taken care of me only to see me the way I am now?
When you entrusted yourself to me, did you know its outcome?
The face of my baby I can't see now I try to see in my mind's eye.

Your pa, who has been waiting for you, goes before seeing you.
Baby, won't you grow up healthy and strong to be 'someone'?
My both eyes are bedimmed and bleary, and I can't see clearly.

Though I've thought of several tricks that'll make you laugh,
Now that I won't see you, all these plans seem to be futile.
I heartily pray that your young soul will attain what I wish.

Last night wet with my love's tears, this dawn with dreary rain!
In a sound sad and dreary a body will be enwrapped.
Two streaks of tears flow down in silence from closed eyes.

* * *

The poplars bragging of their branches wave in the wind,
And charm the onlookers' eyes with their gyrating waists.
Well, I don't envy you for indulging in your being carefree.

To Jŏng-hi

The air was clean and clear, the water welling medicinal.
With pa like a pal, and mom like a loving sister,
I happily grew up in a hut with a low-lying roof.

Chattering like a rivulet flowing down with small ripples,
We walked on, carrying steps light as a maiden's laughter,
Till we passed by the lane whereto we should've turned in.

        *   *   *

I realized only yesterday we'd known each other for ten years.
With no empty words spoken, didn't we know each other's mind?
Many a word was spoken to each other, though few were uttered.

As I ran to the top of the hill covered with dry leaves,
What scenery! The field of Chŏl-won stretched below my eyes!
A young man's impulse to rush on horseback revived again!

We walked six steps in unison to find it futile as we turned back.
When our hearts didn't go together, would our shadows console us?
Watching you walking ahead, I felt sorry to see you limping.

The moon shone on Chŏl-won field bearing Gung-yĕ's dream.[1]
I opened my bleary eyes to see the dim light of an electric bulb;
From the next room came the sound of my sister's breathing.

---

[1] Gung-yĕ (弓裔 ?–918) was the king of Tae-bong (泰封), a kingdom he built and ruled from 898 AD to 918 AD. He was an illegitimate son of King Kyŏng-mun (景文王) of the Shilla (新羅) Dynasty. He ruled the kingdom he had created till it collapsed upon the founding of the Koryŏ (高麗) Kingdom. He is known to have been slaughtered while being chased by the people who supported Wang-gŏn (王建), who built and opened the Koryŏ Dynasty.

Having Bidden Farewell to Jŏng-hi

Why am I watching the candlelight absentmindedly?
Can I daresay I long to be in your warm embrace?
I only want to look on your face, holding your hand.

Knowing it is ridiculous, I cannot suppress tears welling.
People laugh at those who weep, but what is so funny?
Do they consider me foolish? They may very well think so.

I thought I was different from others. How foolish was I!
That the bright moon can cause pain I've known only now!
You, wind, making the boughs weep, pass by with no sound.

The barely audible cockcrow comes from far away.
Has sweet sleep flown away there to be with you?
As only my pillow caresses my cheeks, I feel hollow.

Your face looms in my mind's eye to fill my chest with pain.
As I look into your photo, you seem to be coming back to me.
I wonder how I bade you farewell if I were not to forget you.

You are not a princess. Then why do I act like a prince?
Just like the people appearing in a story, how come we
Remain separated, only longing for each other, I wonder.

Title Lost (VII)

What is your name, you, baby born two days ago?
"My name is Joy." Fluttering his wings, I wish him
To grow up with a pure heart, like a tree.

When my song spreads wide from your heart,
From the crags of dry rocks pure water wells up.
All the chores to be taken care of I've forgotten.

As a morning star twinkles in your smiley eyes,
Sudden blow of a flower looks red between rocks.
The world down there dustless looks like a drawing.

Title Lost (VIII)

How was the pain? It was a dream, now the night is over.
Has there been what they call love? I've almost forgotten.
A new day's light, entwined by wind, circles around me.
                              (On the morning hill)

A Fragment

Whereto is this road leading?
    With what feet does that cloud cross the hill?
        Now the setting sun is lingering over the hill,
            Only the homeless birds are flocking in the sky.

Though you futilely wave your soft wings,
    The blue sky stretches too far and wide to reach.
        The road to tread in dreams goes on forever.
            You feebly wave your soft wings weary and languid.

Get higher and higher till you know no bounds.
    In the boundless sky let the azure jade spread its beam.
        In the crystal-clear well in my heart your face looms.
            I shall feel proud to envision your face cold like a star.

Index

After Sending You off on a Night Train 18
Again 56
As I'm Not Yours 38
Attempt at Composing Four Triplets, An 90
Be Nobler! 36
Being in Love 77
Boat Ready to Set Sail, A 17
Certain Night, A 64
Chance Encounter, A 73
Chilled Forehead 21
Clock That Has Stopped, A 74
Doll, A 75
Downfall Imagined 89
Elegy (I) 85
Elegy (II) 86
Elegy (III) 87
Fairy's Song, The 25
Fracture of the Sky, A 70
Fragment, A 97
Fragment of Thought, A (I) 43
Fragment of Thought, A (II) 44
From Despair 35
Grave and the Moon, A 41
Having Bidden Farewell to Jŏng-hi 94
Heart Soaked with Rain, A 42
Home 22
Hope and Despair 33
Horse I Loved, The 37
I Commit Him to the Flame 54
Invocation 83
Jade Incense Burner, The 88
Jolly Night, A 58
Kite and the Blue Pool, The 66
Lines from 'The Soft Wings' 30

Little Devil, A   29
Love-song, A   49
Mademoiselle Typist   76
Night   65
Night before, The   79
No Title   32
Oblivion   48
Our Nursing Mom (The Boy's Words)   84
Owl is Hooting, An   39
Prayer   82
Rain   24
Rainy Day   34
Renewed Happiness   52
Satyrs   57
Sentimental   51
Shiny Trace   53
Small Sky   71
Snow (I)   63
Snow (II)   78
Snow Falls   61
Song of the Listless Wind, A   67
Though Unable to Go Away Like This   20
Title Lost (I)   45
Title Lost (II)   46
Title Lost (III)   59
Title Lost (IV)   60
Title Lost (V)   69
Title Lost (VI)   91
Title Lost (VII)   95
Title Lost (VIII)   96
To Jŏng-hi   93
Two Birds   55
Upon the Sand on a Moonlit Night   62
Vale of Ten-Thousand Waterfalls, The   81
Whereto?   23
Winter Solstice   47

Words of a Maiden Leaving for a Far-off Place 27
Your Shadow 72

Chronology of the Poet

June 21, 1904: Born in Kwang-san (presently a district of Kwang-ju City), Cholla Province, Korea. His full name was Pak Yong-chŏl (朴龍喆). Later he adopted the pen name 'Yong-a' (龍兒).

Attended Bae-jae High School in Seoul for some time, but withdrew from it in 1920.

While attending Aoyama Gakuin (靑山學院) in Tokyo, Japan, he became a friend of Kim Yŏng-rang (金永郎 1902–1950), and the two poets remained not only lifelong friends but shared spiritual kinship as literary 'purists' believing in the creed of "art for art's sake."

He entered Tokyo School of Foreign Languages (東京外國語學校) in 1923 to study German language and literature, but shortly withdrew from it, and transferred to Yŏnhi Liberal Arts College in Seoul.

In 1930, he created a poetry journal entitled *Shi-mun-hak* (詩文學), together with Kim Yŏng-rang (金永郎 1902–1950) and Jŏng Ji-yong (鄭芝溶 1902–1950). This poetry journal played an important role in opening a new horizon for modern Korean lyrical poetry.

In addition to *Shi-mun-hak* (詩文學), he started publishing two additional literary journals, each in 1931 and in 1933, but could not continue their publications, due to financial difficulties.

He died on May 12, 1938, of tuberculosis.

His posthumous collected writings in 3 volumes were published by the publisher of the poetry journal *Shi-mun-hak* in 1940.

About the Translator

Sung-Il Lee was born in 1943 in Seoul, Korea. He studied English literature at Yonsei University (B.A., 1967), University of California at Davis (M.A., 1973), and Texas Tech University (Ph.D., 1980). He taught at Yonsei University from 1981 till he retired in 2009. Presently he is Professor Emeritus of Yonsei University.

He has published a number of volumes of Korean poetry in English translation, including *The Moonlit Pond: Korean Classical Poems in Chinese,* listed as an Outstanding Academic Book of 1998 selected by *Choice*. He received the Grand Prize in translation in The Korean Literary Awards of 1990, and the 4th biennial Korean Literature Translation Award in 1999, both given by The Korean Culture and Arts Foundation.

www.ingramcontent.com/pod-product-compliance
Lightning Source LLC
Chambersburg PA
CBHW071724040426
42446CB00011B/2208